The EDP method

The E.D.P. Method

John Danen

Published by John Danen, 2024.

THE E.D.P. METHOD

First edition. February 9, 2024.

Copyright © 2024 John Danen.

ISBN: 979-8224982356

Written by John Danen.

Table of Contents

I dedicate this book to my uncle Mochi (dep), to Nandai (the new Frenchman), to Naren, to Daniel, to Maru, to Natalia, to all the people I met in Argentina, to all Argentines and to that great city that is Buenos Aires.

Introduction.

Before explaining the benefits of this new method and its variants, I am going to emphasize a little humility, because otherwise we can go too far. So I'm going to put here a few ideas and concepts that I think you also have to have in your mind to be a little humble and not apply it from the boastfulness and cockiness. All this you have to know also to be a good person and not a conceited boaster, so read all these chapters prior to the method and the method will work better.

The only reality of it all is that you have created your world with your thoughts. By modifying these thoughts you can modify your reality.

The purpose, our purpose, is to love ourselves and create a satisfying world for ourselves, for that we must practice the art of right thinking. We must not deceive ourselves, we must see the reality and the harshness of things. This way we will be prepared for everything that comes our way. There is no greater evil than not being aware of yourself and your situation in the world.

Normally we will be a small thing, one more among hundreds of millions of people and we will lead a normal and ordinary life. No one will know we exist, no one will know we will have died, few will remember us, and almost none will value us, that is the reality of you and everyone else.

There were people who conquered empires, made impressive feats or grandiose discoveries, or led mighty nations, but even those are not remembered. You have to know from now on that you will not be remembered either unless you do something tremendously great. Our glory is ephemeral, fleeting, and insignificant most of the time. This does not mean that if we want to do something important we can't do it, of course we can, we can do anything, but this is what is normal, insignificance, nothingness, we are actually grains of sand on a kilometer-long beach.

Now, within our insignificant and ephemeral life we have to be as happy as we can. I think that we do good by valuing ourselves, because if we do not value ourselves no one will do us any good, they will treat us very badly. That is why before valuing anyone, you must value yourself, even if you are insignificant. We are all here for a cause, and if we are here we are going to contribute to this world trying to shape it according to our interests as much as we can. Sometimes, out of insignificance, the essential thing is that you live happily.

So, yes, you first, of course we do! Who are we going to please, satisfy and pamper more than ourselves? We are our fans, our followers of ourselves, we love ourselves, we like ourselves and we even get excited seeing in the mirror how beautiful we are.

Everything else is superfluous, and although I think it is very good to be charismatic and charming, and that this helps us a lot to relate to others, before all this, what is really important is to love yourself. Also to love those who deserve it, knowing that, many times, that love will not be reciprocated and you will end up being betrayed, even so, we will not care. Everything else is below the important thing, which is that you are happy.

If you like something you do it, if you want something you get it, you should never resign yourself.

We are going to be worshippers of ourselves, caring little for anything outside our interests, because nothing matters so much to us as ourselves and a few very deserving of our affection.

Everything that happens in the world are things that we hear, we regret, we suffer and we want them to be better, but that really, except for things that are very close to us, are things that do not affect us too much. It is better not to see these depressing news, so we are free from being overwhelmed all day long thinking about all the misfortunes that happen. If we have decided to do something to solve this, go ahead, but if we are going to live our little life in our little place, and we do not believe that we can do anything to solve all the problems of the world, we will focus on our little things, leaving this for people with more power than us.

This is not a book for you to be a total bastard, it is simply for you to love yourself more than everyone else, to realize that in life you only have you, and that neither your parents, nor your girlfriend, nor your friends, are going to help you. You have only you, you can only count on you, you have to please yourself. It is a little bit the continuation of "the art of pleasing yourself" but with new and powerful seduction methods. Thus, by seducing, you also please yourself,

It is a book that I felt was necessary, and although everything I say here is a bit narcissistic, what I really want is for people to be happy and to behave well with others, except for very good cause.

If we make ourselves respected, value ourselves and give ourselves the importance we deserve, I even believe that other people will treat us better than being nice to everyone, but not respecting ourselves.

Everything could be much worse.

Imagine you are in a prison in Thailand sentenced to life imprisonment for example, where every day you share a cell with 40 other guys. You are robbed, spat on, beaten and raped by a beast who knows martial arts and weighs 140 kilos. No one will see you, you are hungry and cold, you are sick with a very serious disease, and you don't even go out to the yard, because you have a broken leg and can't walk. In one of the altercations you have been blinded by a punch and you have only three months to live because of your poor health.

You're like this now, aren't you? Then you are fine. You have to be happy because we are not in a situation similar to this, but we are in a more or less normal life, we have friends, we go out and we may even have a wife or girlfriend, and we can even pick up something out there, therefore, we do not have to feel very bad, but feel great, because we are not in one of the worst situations you can be in. So, as long as you are not in a situation like that, you have to always be super happy and grateful to live the life you are living right now.

The poor want you poor.

One day I was going to work, to do my thing, to write my books, to make my videos, to promote myself, in short, to try to carve a path for myself as a writer. This was one more day of my routine in which I had got into, working a lot for many years in a row, sacrificing even what I like the most to be able to prosper, choosing between fun and work, work. Also, a conscientious work, not to work madly, but to know what has to be done and to do it. I was pushing myself to achieve my goals.

Well, that day I was going home to work and on the way I met two men of my acquaintance, they are not bad men, they are not super good either, they are just ordinary men, with rather low aspirations. They were holding me back more than they should have been talking, and I say they are not bad men or anything, but I had to work and I told them, -I'm going, I have to work- then I was surprised by their answer.

- Don't go to work man, don't work, don't you see that you won't get rich?

Hearing this set off all the alarm bells and I thought - what the hell do you know what I'm going to get up to - so I ignored them, said goodbye, left, and went to work.

This is an example of what happens in society, people want you to be like them. If they are in misery and mediocrity and they see that you want to get out of it and be someone, they will want to stop you because they do not feel inferior. They want you to be one more, to put you in their sack of, I don't say losers, but at least, people of the heap without ambition.

So don't listen to the people who haven't made it, listen to those who have, listen to your inner self that tells you to prosper, who are they to tell you what to do?

You must be totally deaf to advice from people without ambition. Set your goals and listen to yourself.

Fools want you to be a fool.

The same as the previous ones, the fools who want fools, people don't want you to stand out, they don't want you to be better than them. That's why everyone will try to sink you, to bring you down to their mediocre level. That's why it's time for you to rebel against this envious society that attacks those who stand out, that you have the balls to set yourself up as the best, the great seducer, and go around well separated from these people who are not going to get anywhere. It's time for you to be the master Seduction.

Don't you like your life, make it better!

If right now you find yourself stuck and frustrated and you think you are going backwards, that your life is not the way you want it to be, it's very easy; stop complaining and get into action to improve it. Do whatever it takes, break up with friends, break up with girlfriends, break up with jobs, break up with everything. You have to have the balls to give up what you have now, take a risk and undertake what you are really looking forward to.

Without sacrifice there is no victory. Without being risky there is no victory. If you stay stuck, if you are comfortable and do not want to make many efforts you will continue to live an unrewarding life. So as I have said many times, draw a plan, set your goals, fight for them, put the discipline and determination you need to put into them. At least put yourself on the road to achieving your goals.

What better way to improve your life than to learn and implement the new seduction methods that I am going to tell you in this book, to become a Master Seduction, a man who really improves his life.

No one will fight for you.

You have the power to change things.

In the end it all depends on you, you are the only one who can change your life. Others do not care what you do, nor will they support it, nor will they understand it, you are the one who knows perfectly how you are and the only one who can make your decisions, the good decisions that satisfy you.

So I don't want you to be affected by what people say. Do what you think needs to be done, you have the power to change things, to go from weakling to strong, from shy to seductive, from poor to rich, from clumsy to skillful.

Only he who believes in himself has the power to change things. Trust in yourself and get to work to change what you have to change.

It's your life and no one knows better than you what you want.

Fucking power guides you.

Not able to change anything? Then make nothing affect you.

If you are not able to change things, then don't complain, you haven't had the balls to fight for what you wanted to be, so you have this life that you don't like but that is the one that corresponds to you because of your pitiful acts. If you are not able to change anything, at least accept what happens to you and be happy living a mediocre life, because this is the life you will have, the one you created for yourself.

Reject it and get a better one, or accept it and don't let it affect what happens to you. Being happy is possible. It is your responsibility to change things, if you don't change them, that's what you have. I know this is hard to hear, but you have to beat consciences to make people better.

An example of all this could be.

I got fired from my job, I don't care, I'll get a better one.

I've been dumped by my girlfriend, I don't care, I'll get a better one, or I won't get one at all and I'll be just fine.

My relationship with my family is bad, it does not affect me, I no longer suffer for anyone or anything.

If you are totally cold hard and detached from everything, then you can be happy with anything and you don't need to achieve great triumphs to be okay, now that's fucking hard!

To be happy, I think it's much better to at least try to really get what you want. Be happy whatever you do.

The mistake of thinking, "If you don't like me, you're an asshole".

Not everyone can like us. Not every girl likes us, not every potential friend likes us, not every job we get.

If you start thinking like this, "if you don't like me you're an asshole for not liking me", then we'll always be pissed off thinking that we don't get what we deserve and that we're a fucking shitty person.

But if we think "even if you don't like him, I'm an asshole, I did like myself", then we'll be just fine because we'll know that the asshole who didn't appreciate us is just that, an asshole, and his opinions have no validity. He has no reason and we don't give a shit about his opinion. We do like ourselves.

He really is an imbecile and imbeciles are not taken seriously, they have no criteria and we should not be bothered by what they say.

Many times people who have power and are listened to and accepted for what they say, do nothing but say wrong things that undervalue us.

But we must also think that this does not always happen, sometimes they are right! and we are not really good for that position, or we do not have what it takes for something. So in these cases, we give them the reason and nothing happens. We start to improve these shortcomings and thank them for discovering them. Other times we are right and they are jerks.

We cannot abuse to think that they are imbeciles, because if we always think like that, the world will be composed of imbecile people who are in charge and who always keep us away from what we want. Let's be reasonable, sometimes they are not wrong, we must be humble and recognize our shortcomings. It is very easy to call everyone a moron and be the only smart one. Use logic, if everyone says you are not worth it, it will be that you are not worth it **at that moment**, nothing happens, you assume it and keep fighting. With willpower everything gets better.

Shielding oneself in a hostile world, where everyone has a grudge against you, is for cowards without self-criticism who live alienated in their unreal world. Many of those who think this are really crazy.

Be smart. Don't fool yourself.

In any case, let's stop worrying about what others think of us. Let's start improving ourselves and loving ourselves despite our shortcomings.

We cannot please them all, not all of them are seduced, otherwise this would be a jauja, a thing so easy that it would have neither emotion nor merit, the fact that there are difficulties, rejections and failures makes the victories more valuable.

If you like me you are smart.

We, in our self-centeredness, tend to think that all people who like or like us are intelligent, and this does not have to be so. There are people who like us who are absolute idiots, who have no personality, and who simply like us, but this does not mean that they are intelligent people.

We create our own world and surround ourselves with sycophants, and this does not mean that these sycophants are right, or that they are smarter, but that we hear what we want to hear.

Generally if you are a magnificent and intelligent person, the people who like you will tend to like you will tend to be like that, intelligent, because like attracts like. But if we are really unpresentable, it will be others of this style that we will attract and they will not be intelligent at all. In this life we want to believe that we are super cool. In reality we are deaf to criticism and super attentive to praise.

Recognize when you're right and when you're being a smug ass who isn't.

If we realize our mistakes and are fair, we will look at ourselves from the outside and see how hard we are to bear and the evil we do, then we will be doing good to the world and to ourselves. To love ourselves is also to recognize our mistakes.

The society of
superficiality.

In this society in which we live, it seems that everything is measured in terms of economic success, wealth, possessions, goods, cars, apartments, motorcycles, houses, stunning women we get, hotels we go to, or meals we eat.

It is believed that happiness is measured by these superficial things that pigeonhole you into this or that social group, but what is really important is that you love yourself and those who deserve to be loved by you. If you are satisfied with your life even without so many luxuries, you will be happier.

You can be a person with very few material things and live very happily, and it could also happen that you are a totally unhappy multimillionaire. Happiness is not in the material and the superficial, but in your mind, in your attitude towards things.

We are in the society of the superficial but we are also touched by this and we take advantage of all this to our advantage.

Even if we are somewhat superficial ourselves, it's okay, we forgive ourselves and enjoy it.

Superficiality ou yeah.

They like me as long as I think the same way they do.

That's right, if you go with a group of friends everything will be fine as long as you think the same as them, but as soon as you disagree on something, give your opinion not according to the rest, they will start to hate you, scold you, and leave you aside, because they will not like to go with you.

People group together with people who think like us, we don't like to hear other versions, it's not nice. If you don't think like them, they will have no mercy in leaving you totally alone, you will be left alone and they will go out partying. Nobody is going to call you because you have upset them.

Many people for fear of this give a false opinion of themselves about everything. They seek to please others and not to suffer rejection. These are cowards who have no personality, because they also do not like to go with people who think differently from them, people who say imbecilities. They have a hard time with them for putting up with such things. So as opinions are like colors, there are many, and you can't be changing your opinion to please others, have the balls for once in your life and give your real opinion. You'll lose those friends you don't like and you'll be able to attract others who will like you. Be authentic.

In the end even with the most like-minded friends there will be disagreements, and they won't be so cool anymore, we will gradually drift apart, until the final breakup. You have to realize this, that no one is going to think exactly like you and that if you both give in a little bit to limits that are agreeable to both of you, you can be friends. But if we break up with everyone who does not think exactly like us, in the end we will be left alone, because not one person thinks the same way about everything as another.

So we must also have a little flexibility and swallow a small percentage of their bullshit, as long as we are not uncomfortable with this, or we will be alone all our lives. Of course, if you don't like them at all, you send them all to hell, but you also have to take into account that the one who goes to hell is you too, because it will be difficult for you to make friends again, and that's how you will always be. You are going to shit because you are alone, but this does not really mean that it is bad, it can be excellent to find yourself and to put your life in order.

Therefore, I believe that we should put up with them as long as they are within acceptable tuning parameters.

That's life, whatever you do, whether you like it a lot or a little, in the end you will end up alone, because I believe that lives are like roads that separate and that all start from an initial point. Those who at ten years old were very close, at 20 will have separated, at 40 they will be far away and at 60 they will be worlds apart. Everything changes, your friends change and you also change with respect to yourself. The you at 40 is not the same as the you at 20.

That people think differently makes anything we achieve more meritorious.

Giving that girl the opportunity of a lifetime.

We think that every girl we pick up is a lucky girl and that we are the chance of a lifetime to be with a great guy. Actually this is what I really think, but I also recognize that I am a bit narcissistic, so the real reality is that, if that girl doesn't go with you there are 50000 others she can go with, and, and this is the most important thing, that once she **has chosen a random one, she tends to reaffirm herself in her choice,** because everybody finds it hard to recognize that she has made a mistake. So even if she doesn't choose you, the girl will be happy with whatever shitty man she goes with, because that's the one she chose and she won't recognize that she was wrong. She's going to persevere and she's going to manage to make herself believe that that's the best one. So even if we really believe we are the best and in our head we are, in reality she will not care if she goes with you or with anyone else, because she will take it for good in her head. It's that crude.

Whether you seduce her or not nobody cares, least of all yourself. No manifestation of our fucking power has the power over us. We have the fucking power, the fucking power, what is manifested we celebrate and what is lost we also celebrate. Fucking power gives us what we need.

The good guys.

This is the problem of us bad boys who dominate and have women at our mercy, that we abuse our position too much. But this does not last forever, little by little the girls get tired of us never letting up and being a little more manageable. We make them suffer too much, in the end sometimes after many years, some lout gets something and takes a woman who is a saint and a good woman, but who has been practically our little toy. We have done with her what we have wanted, he has fallen in love with her like an imbecile and we have only enjoyed her. In the end these poor men persevere and get a woman who no longer makes us any fun, because she is neither a challenge nor anything new. She failed to straighten us out over the years, she was there at our mercy, she tried to be our girlfriend and never went beyond being more than a poorly valued fuck-buddy. Let them enjoy what we do not value, what we always reject. Food that the master does not want, a delicacy for the pig.

Deep down we are happy for the poor girl who finally found a fool who did value her, well, we are generous. Let him eat her with his own bread. We celebrate her loss.

The works.

This really sucks. Generally at work we have to share space with other people that we have not chosen and that are not at all to our liking. These people, better called riff-raff, are the ones we have to put up with every fucking day and it really sucks.

It's been more than fifteen years since I freed myself from working for riffraff, for assholes, for people who treated you badly, who thought they were superior to you. People who are fucking shitty people and you have to put up with all their impertinence because that's what feeds you. This is bullshit and a slavery from which you must get out of as quickly as possible. You will improve your economy by working on other more profitable things, and you will improve your self-esteem by not putting up with these motherfuckers.

If you want to succeed in life you must avoid working for anyone at all costs. Sometimes there are people who are good and we are happy, but an individualistic and cocky guy will never like this. He thinks that you are in a position of inferiority, that if your boss fires you, you go to the street and you are left in misery. Starting from this position of inferiority there can never be a satisfactory relationship, it is an abuse, a hell. That is why here you must like yourself and stand up to anyone who does not like you. Like yourself and do not tolerate any abuse. To get out of this have confidence in yourself and your abilities and make a plan to work for yourself.

Let them go and send someone else.

Sometimes it happens that the bosses are good people and we get along well with them and they treat us well. But it is difficult to like everyone in that office. There will always be the typical buck willing to do anything to please the boss, the typical woman who has not empowered herself at all and who lives there, neglected her family, totally submissive to the boss. The poor man who, like this one, lives to work and does not respect himself in the least. This man will do hours and hours of overtime without ever getting paid anything, and he will barely get shitty recognition. They will all be thrown out mercilessly when it suits, and only the one who makes himself respected, the one who demands his rights, the one they dare not abuse him, for they know he will fight back with all the law, will prevail.

Following this line of thought, and being congruent with myself, I took one of the bosses I had to deal with to court, because of an unpaid salary that he did not pay me. Some people do not have the leadership necessary to work for themselves and prefer this submission, which I do not share at all, but we are not all the same. I think that the salary they pay you is the price to give up your dreams, your ideal life, to be your own boss, to do what you want as you want when you want, to really succeed, to be free. The salary is the price they pay you to buy your freedom.

Although I understand that there are people who want this comfort, I certainly do not share this idea of working for others and here I give you my opinion, then you do whatever you want.

Have partners who understand you and do business together. People who know and help you.

Escape from the woman.

Where I live there is a very handsome guy who is married to a very, very ugly woman with a very unpleasant personality. I often wondered, what the hell did this man see in this woman? After much analysis, I could not come to any clear conclusion other than pure masochism. He is with a woman far below his level and on top of that very unpleasant.

I noticed that this man's hobby was running, and he didn't just run for a little while, he ran for several hours a day, so I understood everything. Before being at home with that horror of a woman, he prefers to be running, and although he suffers a lot, it is less suffering to be running than to be putting up with that woman.

Some people get married and run away from their wives. In any case this is valid for this book, this man created his life this way, with a horrible woman. Things happen! Sometimes there are things that escape me and that I don't understand no matter how many years I have and how much wisdom I acquire. What you can take away from all this is that running is better than being with her.

Why he married that one is a mystery beyond the sharpest minds of mankind. A committee of experts from nasa was assembled along with several Indian personal growth gurus and they came back without any answers totally dejected.

Keep running Forest, go find Buba.

The underpants.

Have you noticed that while they don't have a girlfriend your friends go everywhere with you, and they are even a little heavy, that you never take them off, and that when they get a girlfriend, they disappear as if they had gone to Mongolia, and you don't see them for fifteen years, even if they live two streets away from you?

That's what happens, this friends, is to be a henpecked. When a normal man gets married, he completely disappears for all his friends and gives himself body and soul to his wife. I find it very sad and very unfortunate that these things are done. That out of fear of her, to please her too much, good friends are left behind. I find it outrageous. So to these friends who disappear because of the girlfriend and who reappear again as soon as they lose her, you say to them, didn't you have a girlfriend? Then go with her, you haven't called me in years. We are not here to put up with them when they have nothing to do. You have to take care of your friends, and if you don't take care of them, then, door! Fuck off! Enough of being good and putting up with riff-raff.

You can't please everyone,
please yourself.

Scooter sang an excellent song at the beginning of the century - "you can't please anyone, so please yourself". If you go around pleasing one person, pleasing another, changing your mind to please people, you'll be a wimp and nobody will want to go with you or trust you, because one day you'll say one thing and another day the opposite, depending on who you talk to. You will be a stinker, a guy who you don't know where he is going to come out, you can't trust him.

However, if you are a person who likes himself and says what he really thinks, you will have detractors and you will know who are the people who do not think like you, but you will also have followers. These will be the good people you will like to be with. You will be authentic and appreciated for it. There are a lot of wimps who have no personality and no character. Guys who pretend to please everyone and the only thing they do is to displease absolutely everyone and be disliked by everyone.

Have personality, have your point of view and make it, don't be a pleaser. One of the worst things in life is to be a spineless person who goes around pleasing jerks.

Transition to new methods.

Well I hope that with these initial explanations you have become a little more humble, kind and condescending and also respectful of yourself. Now comes the time to surpass ourselves, to do something never done before, to contradict all the rules of seduction and to be great.

I will now explain the new methods I have developed as a result of my field work.

Everything I tell you I have developed and put into practice successfully, no matter how crazy the actions are, they work! However, I warn you that these new methods require a lot more self-confidence, because they are not so nice methods with girls, but they are dark methods, often challenging and difficult to put into practice. If you do not have a huge self-confidence, they will not work, because many times what I am counting on is to displease the girls, and I know that many will do it wrong and will be quickly expelled from the interaction.

The method is not wrong, the implementation is wrong. If this is done with full fucking power, with self-confidence, with the charm and charisma of the real star, of the one who **believes** he is **really great** and powerful, it works. It is not just apply the method and that's it, you have to do it with the charisma and charm with those weapons almost everything works, even if you are confronting them hard. Really **trust me,** I have done it, I have done wonders, incredible masteries with these methods because I have the self-concept of star well put in my head. You can do it too, it's all a matter of mentalization. Do everything right, if you do it wrong it will give you terrible results.

Use the jd method and when you have mastered it, move on to jd mixed and then to JD dark, when you are comfortable with this method, move on to EDP and finally to EDP dark.

The JD method can be done by almost anyone, it gives results and it is an easy method.

For the JD dark method you need to be much more self-confident, less influenced by their charms, be brave and dare to confront. These dark results will, when this method is done well, be much more powerful than the normal JD.

When we are familiar with the use of the JD dark method and it is giving us results, then we switch to the EDP method and practice and practice with it until we feel comfortable with its use and it gives us good results, and finally we switch to the EDP dark method.

Before you had only one method, throughout 23 books I only developed one, here in this book I develop four new ones.

This life happens and if you don't have the courage to behave the way you would like to behave, to be someone magnificent, to be the star, to be someone special, to be proud of yourself and your triumphs, who the fuck is going to do it? It's your fucking life, it's your responsibility.

The time is now, this is your life, if you do not do what really makes you illusion you will be a failure all your life. This EDP method allows you to be the star, to shine, to reach very high, take advantage of it.

All this, as crazy as it may seem, I do it for them and for you, because they like it that way, because being nice too much they don't like us, because they like the guy who tells them no, and that is a challenge for them.

With all this what I want is that women enjoy and have a good time, I am a defender of them and although with the methods they are pricked a little, this is superficially, we never make them a serious offense, but we play with them, pricking them a little, deep down we are their great defenders, we love them, we want and respect them. That's why we give them what they say they don't want but need, what they really want, the charming bad boy who makes them rage and drives them crazy with love. The Master Seduction.

Female masochism.

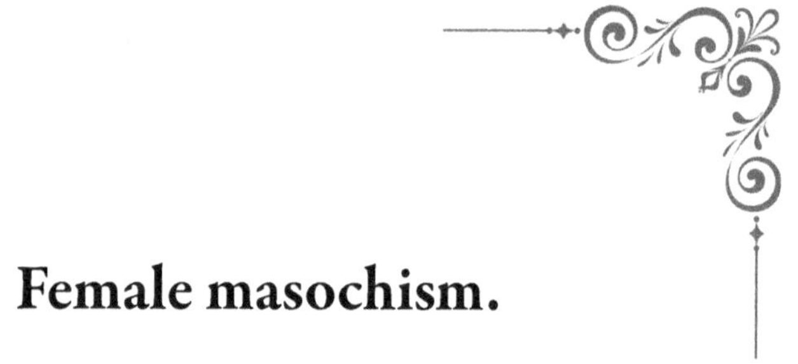

It was precisely a woman, called Helene Deutsch, who wrote several scientific works where she defended that women were masochists, that is to say, that they liked to suffer. This was not done by a man, nor a male chauvinist, or anything like that, it was a woman disciple of Freud, who wrote in 1930 "The significance of masochism in female mental life", she also wrote "Psychology of women" in 1945. She will know why she said this, but it was certainly not just anyone who said it, but a very reputable psychologist. These works are of course not shown to people today because they are not politically correct, but they are there whether they like it or not.

Based on these scientific works and above all on the experience that proves them right, I build my methods. I really believe in this truth, yes, I think they are masochists, not to the fullest, but a little masochistic yes. To get the answer as to why this masochism you will have to read the works of this woman. She will know.

So if scientists say so for a reason, we will use this weakness to our advantage.

We will be a little bad, but deep down, good, we will use these weapons, but we will never really despise them, nor treat them badly, it is all a game to attract them to us. We, the seducers, are the great defenders of women and the ones who care the most about them and their needs. We sacrifice ourselves for them, and if we have to be bad, then we are bad, because that way they like us more, everything is always for them.

The scientists have spoken, I have nothing more to add.

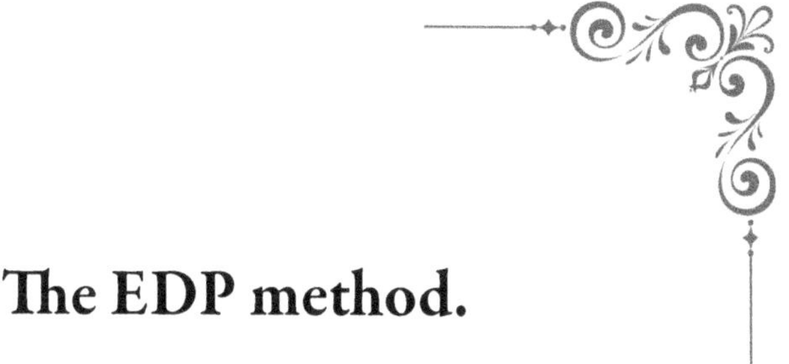

The EDP method.

This method is an evolution of the JD method for those who have reached excellence. It is a method that not everyone can use because it requires a high level of seductive qualities. You do things that do not seem rationally good to seduce. But when you position yourself strongly by mastering this method, the actions you develop, work.

The JD method is an easy and simple method, it is applicable to any interaction and will give results very quickly. It is the method that you should use more often. It is a method with which girls will like you and you will be liked.

This other method the EDP is for the braver people, people who don't mind confronting, even displeasing the girl a little, people who want to risk and have more impact. People who know that it is a slower method than the jd method, although this slowness does not always happen only in some occasions, there are others in which the impact is immediate. Also a much greater impact than with the JD method.

Why do girls want the star?

Being someone important, or at least someone with a position, or knowledge, or life different from the rest, makes you be appreciated as better.

Let's not fool ourselves, girls want the star, the Hollywood actor, the famous guy on TV, the singer, that one is pre-selected above all others and is perceived as better than the rest.

This is why I have included this parameter in this method, because if you are perceived as the best, or at least someone very good at something, you will be more valued and even admired, and we can use this in our favor to seduce.

Why do they like a distant star?

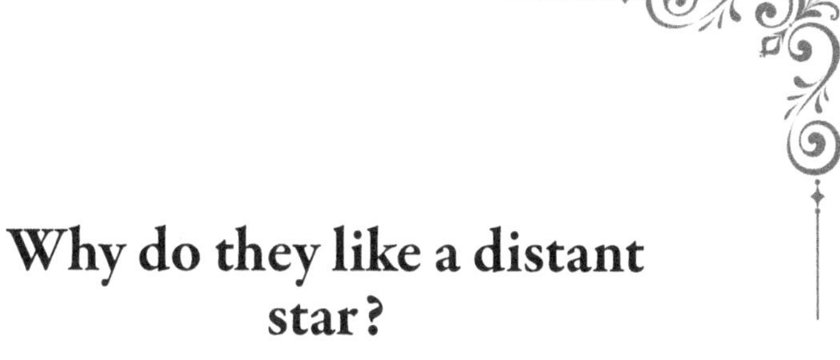

People, not just girls, are looking for someone unattainable, someone above their capabilities and above their comfort zone, so this star has to be aloof, has to be something quite large and taller than the others she usually interacts with.

I am not referring with this word distant to you being someone cold, but to you being far out of their reach, a distant star, far above their level.

To achieve this is not easy at all. That's why you must look for what capabilities make you unique and special, to be the star in something, a star so high that it is also distant. This stardom you will have to be able to demonstrate it, you will have to give him proof that you really are that distant star, or he will not believe you.

Look for what you are the best at, what sets you apart from the rest, and if you have that use this advantage to your advantage and be the distant star. Once you have found it sell yourself well and tell him the advantages of your stardom.

If you don't have anything that sets you apart from the rest, something that can make you be perceived as the star, then I'll tell you one thing, you can acquire something that sets you apart and positions you above everyone else in a really powerful subject like seduction.

You can be a Master Seduction if you take the Master Seduction video course. Then you will have your stardom, something that differentiates you from others, you will be a seducer with an official diploma that qualifies you as a Master Seduction.

This qualifies you as a distant and dangerous star and you must communicate this to her with a certain humility, without boasting. She must know that you are a star of seduction, even if you do not yet have huge amounts of success, you will soon have them by applying these teachings from the course. You have the knowledge.

You are also a rather tall, aloof and even dangerous star. You will be able to tell her that you have taken the best seduction course in the world and that it has been validated by John Danen himself. These special abilities that make you superior to the rest when it comes to seduction, you will subtly communicate them to her, until you finally reveal the whole truth.

Why are you dangerous?

You are dangerous because your capabilities are like those of a martial artist, but instead of fighting, in love. You are validated and have received a diploma as someone very powerful in the field of love. So these abilities of yours could be dangerous for her, because she can easily fall in love with you. As the diploma certifies, apart from being seductive you are also tough and charming, so she runs the risk of falling in love and may suffer. You are going to be kind and not allow her to suffer, but she runs a risk.

So you're a star, you're also aloof because you're a high-level star and you're also dangerous to her. You warn them of your capabilities and you show disinterest in flirting with them because you don't want to abuse your capabilities, because they could get hurt if you don't measure your enormous attractiveness. This dangerousness and distancing, even in some cases prohibition that you make them to be with you, is what attracts them to you.

Girls are turned on by the forbidden and even knowing that you are a womanizer and probably a bad boy, they will want to be with you. They like the forbidden, the dangerous, the exciting, they don't like the usual, the normal, the usual.

When they meet a Master Seduction they meet someone very skilled in love and highly seductive, this will be a challenge for them. You will also join your stardom in some other field that you can demonstrate that will make you even more challenging, the target to achieve.

You will be uninterested in flirting with her, you will be the challenge, the difficult man to get, the man who doesn't want to go with her because he's into other things, someone who knows he is very powerful and that doesn't suit her very well because she could fall in love with you.

This status as a distant and dangerous star creates an aura of challenge that motivates them to conquer you.

Here we play with the concept of hybristophilia. This concept says that some women are attracted to dangerous characters. We are not criminals or really dangerous guys, but we can become slightly dangerous because of our knowledge and enormous attractiveness. They may be a little afraid to fall in love with us because we are not the good guy. This concept is slightly exploited in this method and in general in all dark methods.

The EDP method.

This method is a cocky and challenging evolution of the JD method. Using this method the interaction will be enjoyable, except at rare moments.

We show ourselves unconcerned about flirting with her and we place ourselves above her subliminally. This method as I have already said is a more risky method, more cocky and challenging, and you should use it if you want to risk more, if you want to have a strong hit and do things slowly and well. The effects are more powerful than with the JD.

I think that its success rate is lower, but its hit rate is higher, that is, you will have fewer successes than with the JD, but those that are affected by these new actions will fall irremediably.

The name of this method comes from these initials:

E for star

D for distant

P for dangerous.

I am going to tell you why I invented this method and how I found out that it works, then I will tell you in detail each of the actions that make up this method.

We will slightly use in our favor the hybristophilia and also the female masochism. These two issues are proven scientific issues.

How did I realize this?

I have always known that women like the most valuable, the unattainable, they fall in love with their rock idols, presidents of governments, famous and illustrious people, people who appear on television, people who are experts in something. In short, people they deeply admire.

This power of attraction that they feel towards these people, considered experts or stars, is key to their pre-selection.

We must be someone very great, someone they admire, and, far from hiding it, show these capabilities, this power, this something that surprises and admires them.

It goes without saying that a Hollywood actor will be super well seen by them and does not need to use any method, since he is already famous and recognized by all. We don't have such cache, but with this method we will get a little bit closer to the privileges that these people have.

I have also realized that women are attracted to the forbidden and also to the dangerous, so if we combine being an expert in something, being someone important in a subject, with the forbidden and dangerous, we will be generating a lot of attraction simply with these two characteristics.

Hannibal Lecter said that we desire what we see, but I add that we also desire the forbidden, the dangerous, the unattainable, the higher level. Therefore we will use this psychological preference to benefit from it.

Many years ago, the Frenchman, the matador and I were with some girls, and since we felt so powerful and sure of ourselves, instead of trying to pick them up, what we did was to laugh, telling them crazy things and answering their questions in a totally shameless way.

One of them asked me.

John, are there any controls to go to your town? (Referring to breathalyzer controls made by the police to see if you have drunk alcohol), I answered him

-Yes, don't worry, there are controls, Durex, Prime, I have everything.

She was a little frightened by this shameless answer and then asked the Frenchman.

-And what do you do for a living?

The Frenchman replied all serious with his Parisian accent.

-We dedicate ourselves to **making love.**

The woman was hallucinating, so she looked at the matador to see what he was saying and the matador added

-Yes, to make love, the strange thing is that we are not doing it yet.

All this boasting and cockiness, not only didn't scare them too much, but I think it seduced them, we met up with them for another day and I hooked up with one of them, who was one of the prettiest on my resume, and with great ease. Despite doing all these crazy things they were receptive, so that's when I realized that being a star works, especially if you add a touch of humor.

I also realized that a profession or activity that is considered as a person of great experience in love, gives you a position of a star, of someone dangerous because of his enormous knowledge.

While I was in Argentina filming the Master Seduction course, when I was interacting with the girls and they asked me what I did for a living, I would tell them

-I am a seduction coach," this made them hallucinated and interested in me.

Many of them flirted shamelessly, so I realized that this worked and it did work. I realized that this status as a seduction star, as a coach, as someone who is perceived as powerful because of his skills, especially in love, gave a lot of power over girls and attracted them.

That's why you will also be a star, a certified Master Seduction, and you will attract them by making this status known.

You can also say that you are dedicated to love, to seduce girls, to flirt, tell them this without any fear or regard, this will also impress them because you are sincere, brave and defiant.

The EDP method itself.

This method, of course, is a variation of the JD method, a much more evil variation. You will only be able to use it if you have mastered the JD method to perfection, as it requires more nerve, more brazenness, more shamelessness and much more security.

We will start, of course, talking about the internal game, this is absolutely the same as in the jd method, with the only difference that you see yourself in this new superior role and your visualization will be much stronger than in the jd method. Later I will detail an example of correct visualization.

Deployment in the EDP method:

Fun.

Of course, we will start with the most important action for this method and for everyone, fun. There is no variation here, you will be a super fun and cheerful person who has a great time, and who conveys a happy world where she is welcomed, accepted and valued.

Even though you know of your enormous power, you are kind and you bring her into your world, because even a star like you is nice, why shouldn't you be nice? You are happy in your world of success and you make her participate in it, you make her laugh and have a wonderful time. These actions to make her laugh you must practice with your own style, use your wit and creativity to say things that reinforce the festive atmosphere of joy and fun in which you are immersed. That's it, you must always practice it at the highest levels and create your own style. The more you master humor, the more you will be able to put up with your cockiness later on.

Uninhibited.

We will be uninhibited as in the JD method, but this time even more so. This time this disinhibition will be a little bit stronger. This disinhibition will be very strong and we will talk about any topic, no matter how controversial it may be. The more our conversation is contrary to her ideas the better, the more we will be independent, indifferent and unconcerned about flirting with her. This makes her uncomfortable and it's bad, but that's the way it should be. We are going to make an impact, to be badass, to please almost nothing at certain moments.

Unconcerned.

We will continue with the nonchalance of flirting with her, exactly as in the JD method, we will be nonchalant about being with that girl as she is not the object of our love interest or sexual interest. We will simply be there with her emanating our attractiveness, being witty and being in an interaction most of the time pleasant for both of us, but without any intention to seduce. We will never despise her, but if we can attack things, we will be there playing with her as a lion plays with a little mouse.

Comfortable.

The next action is to create the comfort she so badly needs in order to be with you. This comfort has to be magnificent and of a much higher level than what is done in the JD method, as she is also much more uncomfortable.

We have blown her mind, she has been rejected and little about us, but now we are going to be great party partners, we are going to make her laugh, we are going to care about her, be attentive, be nice, be real charmers and we are going to make her feel great by being very nice to her.

We even go, to relativize and minimize the statement, prior leaving the door open to love and giving her the reason also in her arguments to please her a little, if we see that she is too uncomfortable or annoyed. She knows that she is not the object of our interest, but she feels comfortable with us.

This method is of great masters who don't really care about failure or success, Master seductions who are really playing with girls and who are able to assume that some of them don't like us and despise us.

She feels super comfortable, we are very attentive and even flatter her on occasion.

We do not use Complicidad, or we use it very little. It does not appear as official lyrics.

We do not use Descaro, and if we do use it, it is to refer to others, but very little or none at all.

Star.

But not content with that, we will do even more brave deeds. Little by little we will reveal our true identity, we will do this if she asks us something like this

-What do you want, or what are you looking for, or what kind of relationship do you want, or are you formal, or are you looking for a fling, or what kind of relationship do you want, or are you formal, or are you looking for a fling?

We will tell you.

I am a Master Seduction, a person who is dedicated to seduce women, I am someone who is hard to fall in love with, because although I can be charming, I am dedicated to this, to seduce, I belong to the community of Master Seduction seducers and I am really different from the rest.

I am a good person but I think I do not suit girls if they are looking for a formal guy. I'm not looking for a serious relationship, because that's not what I usually look for, although sometimes I also have serious relationships, I'm a seducer who seduces until he finds true love. I owe myself to seduction, to this life of emotions. For a long time I have led this life that is very satisfying and has brought me to you. I do not want to seduce you, I simply want you to know that it is difficult for me to fall in love and perhaps I am not the right one for what you want, which I think is love.

Having made this shocking statement, she will be apparently horrified or maybe she has already taken effect so much cockiness and so much sincerity and is being attracted terribly unintentionally.

This statement would have even more power if you were a seduction coach, seduction book writer, porn actor, or anything that is challenging to her, but even without being all that, being a Master Seduction will sound very powerful to her and give you credence as a seducer.

After this statement we will have devalued it by not making it our objective.

We have taken her out of the spotlight. We are in the business of seduction and she will feel lesser than you because even though you like seducing so much, you are not doing anything to please her, nor to seduce her, so you have positioned yourself as more valuable than her, both for your experience and for your statement on the limit of what is bearable.

All this will be enough to create an enemy for us if we leave it at that, but now we will show all our charm as shameless seducers and attract her, once we have weakened her with this shocking statement...

Kind.

Finally we treat her like a little sister that we protect, we pamper and care for her. We are the loving and nice protector, we are effusive, we hug her, we value her, we consider her a wonderful girl, we tell her that she is a hottie, that she is super beautiful, but we have no love interest in her.

Here we are very different than in the JD method, with this action we are treating her in a loving, paternal, kind way, we recognize her merits, we tell her how wonderful she is. I learned this from my uncle Mochi who was affectionate, nice and super appreciative with the girls.

He would tell them that they were cute, great and fantastic and made them feel very good. And from time to time he would also belittle them a little by making funny jokes like calling them little monsters, he was the ultimate representative of the school of charisma. He was up there at the top shining, being affectionate, protective, charismatic, making the girls and everyone around him feel great, with an impressive wit and witty banter.

He grabbed them a lot, even kissed them on the face and had them gawking with awesome power. You have to have that charisma to make her feel wonderful. Uncle Mochi's teachings will not be in vain, I will take up his baton and tell you what it takes to seduce.

I have never seen anyone with so much charisma and power of attraction, he was the party itself and made everyone feel good who was with him. A great man from whom we should learn that magnificent charisma.

We are super charismatic, charming, fantastic, unique and special, but unfortunately we are not for those things. You're a Master Seduction who doesn't want that girl to fall in love with you.

You also imply that we are a little afraid of love, that we try, under the guise of seductive, not to get too involved, because deep down we are weak and fall in love too. So this supposed weakness of ours has to be interwoven with our kind actions, they must think that deep down it is all a facade what you do, because you are afraid of love. This will bring them more to you as they will see what you are really good at.

Suddenly we will see clearly the signs of her evident attraction to us. We should not be in a hurry, it is she who will come to us and that day we will be kind and give her what she secretly desires and does not dare to ask for, what she is afraid of, what is a challenge, what is forbidden, the bad boy, the sincere guy who does not hide what he is, the charismatic seducer who does not want to seduce her. The master seduction

In the end the letters are:

D fun

D uninhibited

D carefree

C comfortable

E star

B kind

D optional blatant if after several days if the method really failed.

Since it is a lot of letters and a lot of mess, I center the name of the method on the star, a Distant and Dangerous Star.

Be kind.

After so many stars, we have to put our feet on the ground and prove that we are good. This will make them feel tender.

You have to be kind but like a father to his children, or a big brother to his little sisters. A loving, protective and friendly kindness. After having done all those bad things and having positioned yourself so superior, now you do this paternalistic attitude that also positions you as uninterested in flirting with them, above their reach. We are charismatic, pleasant, kind, playful and above all warm and protective. Here we can play a lot with physical contact, embrace and protection that is given without any amorous or sexual intention.

As soon as you detect the signs of attraction you know you have won. Little by little you become kind and close.

Closing with the EDP method.

When you realize that the girl is with you comfortably laughing at you and very close to you, then it will be the right time to close.

It is necessary to take advantage of the peaks of mood to close. When the mood is high take the opportunity to hug her, in any of these hugs can fall the kiss.

With this method what we have tried is to attract her, now she is attracted and even touched by our kindness, obviously we realize it and we close.

If she really isn't attracted enough, then we'll use the wild card of sass.

I actually don't recommend it too much that you use it, if you are above, you are above you should be consistent with your star position, continue with comfort and charismatic goodness.

Only if the method has really failed can we use chutzpah as a last attempt at closure.

I would let a few days pass and not be in a hurry to close.

The EDP Dark method.

Thinking and thinking I have realized that there may be variations on this method, and even on the JD method, as I will tell later. The first variation is this, the EDP Dark method.

In this method we will do the same things as in the normal version: we will be funny, uninhibited, carefree, stars, comfortable and finally kind, but we will add one more ingredient that will displease them. This is going to have a major effect on their psyche and give us great power over them. This new action is called confronting.

Confronter.

We are going to confront the things you say even if we are not really like that, nor think like that, we will do this to weaken them. We must do it in a light-hearted way and not be a harsh confronter which would turn them totally against you.

It seems very crazy that in order to seduce you have to confront, but this is similar to what people often do to seduce, which is to mess with the person they like a little bit, they do this to tease them, to annoy them, to weaken them. That's the key, confrontation weakens and makes you be perceived as different from everyone else they praise. Slightly hated, but we already know that from love to hate.

I'm not much of a fan of doing this because I find it a bit of an overly arrogant and unpleasant person, but you can do it moderately and then sweeten it.

With this we will show that we are not to please, we do not care what she thinks of us. We are to other things more important than her, we do not care much what she thinks or says about us. We give our opinion whether she likes it or not, especially if she doesn't like it, this will turn her against us and will make her a little angry to see that we are someone who sometimes displeases her, you are not there to laugh all her thanks and to say yes to everything.

We have to do this in a very measured way or we will be seen as imbeciles. We will be a person who is not there to please but to speak our truth whether we like it or not. Although it may seem unbelievable this confrontation will attract her, because we will be someone who is not affected by her or her beauty, We dare to confront a hottie that everyone says yes to please.

We will be confrontational, we will be at the limit of what is assimilable and we will not go beyond that, otherwise she will tell us to leave, or she will leave, or she will not want to talk to us.

We will confront but we will not go beyond that line, finally we will say that we respect your opinion but we do not share it and that is democracy, to think differently.

With this we will be someone totally different from the rest. Let me give you an example. One said she was a fan of a certain soccer player, I didn't care, I'm not interested in soccer, but I saw her weakness and I confronted her with that.

I did this because I was cocky, because I didn't feel like pleasing her, because I felt like being bad, to fuck her and also because I wanted to experiment to see what would happen, so I did it. I already knew that these confrontations cause them a psychological impact and leave them vulnerable, because I had done it once when the thing had come out like that by chance, that time I saw the great weakness that this caused her after being confronted.

So in this case of the soccer player I told him that he was a kid who earned millions and did not really do anything intellectual, I told him that he had no charisma, that he looked like a nice guy, but that he had nothing to admire, that the man who attended his store who earned little money, or the policeman who directed the traffic, was more admirable.

This confrontation caused the expected impact, she felt out of her princess frame, she felt that I was no longer the prize, that I was not there to please her and that I was a different guy, independent and tough. She immediately started making body language that I quickly decoded as attraction to me.

Create confrontation, displease her, show yourself totally distant from her ideas, and finally whitewash yours by being more polite and understanding of her position as well.

With all this we will be displeasing her and making her see that we are not there to please her or to seduce her, but that we are a man with our ideas very clear, a guy who is not intimidated or adapts to what she wants or likes. These attacks weaken them, make them feel vulnerable, and this, incredible as it may seem, makes them sensitive, soft and romantic. You confront her, which no one else does, and now she treats you better, precisely because of this confrontation you have made.

Also once many years ago I had a confrontation with a woman I entered and she said or did something that displeased me very much, then instead of taking the matter down, I reproached her and criticized her, this left her shocked, she became less aggressive, more sensitive, soft, kind and apologized, then I noticed her affected and with a propensity to a good evaluation of me precisely because of that, for confronting, for being a tough guy who makes himself respected.

You can say the phrases -I don't care what you think of me-, or -I don't care what you think, or, I'm not here to please you, I say what I think.

On the outside she will dislike you very much, but inside you will leave her touched, it is then a matter of softening this to really attract her.

If the confrontation has been excessive and she is very angry, then you tell her that it was all a joke. In this case you will have been an asshole who has displeased her too much and you have had to back down. You will have done it very badly, it is not about the girl getting totally defensive or offended, it is about small confrontations, small things, that many times, if we see that we have done her an excessive aggravation, we say that they are jokes.

I don't like to do this in excess, not even to do it, but since I am innovating, creating new seduction systems, I have to tell it because it really works. Don't confront her too much, but if you use this technique don't fall short either, use humor, take the iron off everything you say afterwards, understand her and finally be very kind to make amends for all this confrontation.

Then the EDP Dark method looks like this:

Fun.

Uninhibited.

Unconcerned.

Comfortable.

Star.

Confronter.

Comfortable again.

Kind, protective and affectionate type.

It will take time for her to be seduced, as it is a slightly more long-term method, but she can sometimes be seduced at the first interaction.

How are the EDP and EDP Dark methods applied?

These methods only work if the girl can be seen on more occasions, that is to say if we have a telephone or contact, or if we know where to find her regularly. After this first contact so shocking we will make the whole evening magnificent for her and we say goodbye in a gentlemanly and attentive way so that she feels good, because these actions that make her feel bad must be done very little time because they are very shocking, while the rest of the time, we will be magnificent and nice men attentive to her and even slightly gentlemanly.

The attack we made on her weakened her defenses, made her feel vulnerable and that vulnerability was created by you with your confrontation, then you were even more boastful and placed yourself on such a superior plane that she felt little, then we made amends with our magnificent performance as nice gentlemen being comfortable and kind.

We say goodbye to her without any intention of closing and **leave her forgotten**. This is important, we will wait for her to show signs of life, if she does nothing we will let a week go by for our next interaction. This will show that you are on to other things, that you have other concerns. And it really will be so, your other concerns will be to do the same to many others, whom you will also leave forgotten.

You leave them alone and they come back to you. They come back because you have become a kind of neutron star or black hole that attracts them, irremediably. This is different from what everyone else does and if you have been a little unpleasant and then very pleasant, you will have done the EDP or EDP dark method well and they will call you and want to see you.

When you see them you can talk to them about other girls that you hit on or about your life without rest as if they were your friends, without worrying at all about seducing them, all this will leave them in shock and the day will come when you will be with her as a good friend, but in this case you will not be the good friend who is below them, but the good friend who is far above them.

You will notice her proximity, her gaze, gestures of obvious attraction to you and as we have been bad, punishing, cocky and boastful, despite trying to be humble, we will now be kind and give her what she secretly desires and does not dare to ask for. That day we will give her what she needs, we will give her ourselves, then we will apply the B of kind and kiss the girl. She will fall fulminated because she already knows who you are and it is almost certain that that same night you will also sleep with her because this delivery that she makes now will be total.

And more or less this is the EDP and EDP dark methods, now I am going to go a little deeper by giving examples explaining each of the actions correctly so that you understand it well and do not make a bad performance.

In your head you must have the happy state, always be happy, even if you confront and go as a star, be concerned about her, worried about her welfare, not to hurt her, because deep down you are good and you want that girl not to suffer, that's why you don't offer yourself, that's why you don't go to her, that's why you try to take her away from you.

I think these methods are of enormous power and if the girl is sufficiently attracted you create very good bonds, because you have been her protector, you have warned her, and still she has given herself. You will be very kind to her. She is a brave girl who, despite knowing that you are a man who is dedicated to what he is dedicated to, appreciates that you behave well with her and that you do not lie to her.

In the end, love may even arise because this girl who is going to give so much can soften you because you see that you really are a good person. In your speech should also be underlying the idea that deep down you are looking for love, but to find it you maximize the number of girls you meet, so you will find it faster. Deep down we are sensitive and good. If we like this girl very much then we will tell her that for her we leave all our dedication because we have already found the ideal girl and we concentrate on her, because she is someone special. So, with these rather problematic actions, love can also arise.

You must also make your statements credible. If you tell her that you are a seducer, that you are dedicated to seduce and then she sees you needy, soft, and insecure, or unattractive, she will not believe you.

It is important that you transmit your qualities well, so that they do not doubt that you really are a Master Seduction. Therefore, to give more credibility to your statement, when you do the Master Seduction course, you will be given a diploma that certifies you as a Master Seduction, and you can show it to this girl.

This seems a bit crazy, but it works, I do not recommend you to be doing it all the time, it is better to use the JD method, only some time when you feel like experimenting, be much harder and seduce in a more risky way, you can do this method. If you do it well you will achieve a much more convincing triumph than with the JD method. He who does not risk does not win.

It's important not to be all the time bragging about your seductions and being an arrogant jerk. You just have to mention it a little bit and not be all the time being proud and boastful about it. You have to enhance the comfort a lot because also the attack and attraction that you have made is much stronger, and if you go too far she will reject you outright, and call you a jerk or whatever. You know, you know this can happen. It can also happen what I have told you, that she will fall in love and lose. The result will depend on your good game, not on the method itself, which is quite reliable.

Certainly don't say it to a feminist or someone like that, but don't be afraid to use it either.

You must be humble, willing to help the girls, willing to be positive for society, don't sell yourself as a predator. Show yourself as someone who is an expert in love as if you were a black belt karate man who has a martial arts school, or who is a master in a very good martial art. Warn them, but don't brag about it. Be humble and kind to the girls. You can also vary this confrontation quite a bit depending on which girl it is, if you overdo it you will be perceived as being mean, if you underdo it you will not make the emotional impact on her that weakens them.

The EDP method can and should be regulated in intensity. We will not apply the star and danger in all its rawness if the girl is very fearful. Because she can be mean and fearful. Going star can be adapted and sometimes this star has nothing to do with seduction, we will do this for fearful girls who we know would not stand such an exhibition. This stardom should not be removed as a seducer, more than in very special cases, in which we will be a stock market investor, an expert in cryptocurrencies, a successful entrepreneur, or anything that is difficult to prove, because it will be a lie most of the time.

The dangerousness we will also adapt it, but it can never be omitted, if it is with fearful girls then this dangerousness will be minimal and we will allude to the fact that, in its day, we flirted a lot, or, that it is in danger of falling in love as it happened to some ex of ours.

The EDP method allows us to lower the intensity, but never to eliminate the star, which will be the seduction star in 90% of the cases. The dangerousness will always be related to your seduction capabilities, if we remove the star and the dangerousness we would be applying the JD light.

The more bad they are, the more star and the more dangerous we say we are, or at least we have been, and the more danger we warn them that they run.

Whatever method we use, when we see something we don't like, we confront. We make Dark to that method. Never overlook the possibility of confrontation. The meaner they are the more you have to confront. They themselves ask for their dark dose according to how they treat us.

The EDP method is to overwhelm, let's risk, let's be daring, this is very valid for bad girls. To these girls that we bring down from their pedestal with our stardom, we do them good by confronting them. For kind girls the JD is better.

Try to use it with high, and sometimes even sky-high, seduction star loads, and a lot of danger. You are good-natured, a good-natured sometimes feigned to reduce cockiness, but if you have to confront you confront, even strongly.

Confrontation is a dark action that was already said with other words in Dark seduction. This confrontation makes dark seduction also useful in the process of flirting.

The nerve.

S ass should be discarded from this method because if we are a star how are we going to go after it by being sassy. Stars and even more if they are dark have a very high self-esteem and do not try to seduce the women they are with, but what they do is to attract them to themselves.

If someone uses the EDP or EDP dark method, and also adds sass to it, they are doing a pretty crazy thing, going all star and confronting her in the dark case, it's pretty uncomfortable, and then being sassy with her.

I believe that this would be a total mistake, because we have offended her too much and after this offense she needs some time to heal her wounds, and to be attracted to us with our charismatic attitude. An attitude also comfortable and even kind to her, after such actions.

If we are cheeky on top of that we will be, I think, offending too much, and we will not seduce her at all, it will be an inconsistency and a serious mistake, so do not think of adding cheekiness to any of these methods. For they already carry the cockiness components too high and do not admit any more cocky actions. Both work indirectly and over a rather long period of time.

The JD dark method.

We already have two new methods, now I am going to release a third one, the JD dark, which together with the JD method, will make a total of four seduction methods.

The JD method can be used in direct or indirect style. I don't know why I feel like being a bit mean and I'm going to fix some small flaw that the jd method still has.

In the JD method we have.

Fun.

Uninhibited.

Unconcerned.

Comfortable.

Accomplice.

Discharged if necessary

It is a quick method that generates attraction, good vibes, good atmosphere, the girl likes you and you are someone nice, a little indifferent on occasion, but nice, because we are always charismatic. But what would happen if we remove the complicity, which is really a softness, it's really something we do to bond with her, something that gives away our intentions to flirt with her, and if, instead of complicity, we use confrontation, a small and moderate confrontation mixed with humor?

I believe this enhances the method and makes us be seen as meaner, more arrogant, more unconcerned about flirting and ultimately, more attractive.

So I am not going to repeat the whole method, but simply tell you that you can use the JD method in its Dark version by applying the confrontation, as I explained above.

Then the JD dark method looks like this.

Fun.

Uninhibited.

Unconcerned.

Comfortable.

Confronter.

Comfortable again.

Discharged if necessary

In this order would be fine. Don't take too long to apply comfort or too much cockiness will push her too far away and then you won't be able to create enough.

Once confronted, take the heat out of your confrontation and return to comfort.

I think the JD method in this dark variant is even more powerful, because you have that debilitating effect that confrontation gives you.

Use it with cool women, women who are a little overconfident, to lower their high self-esteem.

For kinder women, the regular style JD method is best.

With this variation the JD method joins the dark seduction and becomes a dark JD method, more malevolent but I think with more punch.

I think this JD dark method is the second best method of all.

In the ranking of which method is better, I think it's like this:

- Mixed JD method, which I explain as follows
- JD dark method
- JD Method
- EDP Method
- EDP dark method

The mixed JD method

The JD method can be applied in dark mode or in normal mode. You can also **mix both** and use complicity in some moments and confrontation in others, experiment, use light and dark weapons.

I think this method is the best of all.

Fun.

Uninhibited.

Unconcerned.

Comfortable

Confronter/ accomplice.

Comfortable again.

Discharged if necessary

Be sometimes good and sometimes bad. Reward and punish, dominate the interaction.

If things go the way we like, we create complicity; if things go the way we don't like, we create confrontation. Let's be great, let's take things where we want them to go.

This is the best possible method of seduction, it is super important I don't explain anything here because it is already explained by everyone else. Always use this method.

New methods.

Now we have the EDP method, the EDP dark method, the jd method and the JD dark method and the JD Mixed method.

EDP method EDP method dark JD method JD method dark Mixed JD method

Fun Fun Fun Fun Fun Fun

Uninhibited Uninhibited Uninhibited Uninhibited Uninhibited

Unconcerned Unconcerned Unconcerned Unconcerned Unconcerned

Star Comfortable Comfortable Comfortable Comfortable

Comfortable Star Accomplice Confrontador Confrontador/complice

Kind-hearted Confrontational Cheeky Comfortable Comfortable

Comfortable Shameless Shameless

Kind

In both PDCs, after a period of time it is possible to be Discarded if necessary.

EDP methods are slower methods and JD methods are faster. Your experimentation must be like this:

- JD.
- Mixed JD.
- JD dark.
- EDP.
- EDP dark.

Errors implementing EDP, EDP dark and JD dark and JD mixed methods.

Excessive confrontation.

If we do this the girl will be offended and then even if we try to be kind, to say, to say that it was a joke, you will not be able to remove iron to the matter and we will have screwed up with our excessive confrontation.

Insufficient confrontation.

If we confront her very little and immediately say that it is a joke or it is a very light thing that we say, we will not really have confronted her and it will be noticed that we do this confrontation simply to mess with her because we like her. So we are not confronting anything, nor are we tough guys, the JD or EDP methods in their dark versions will not work well.

Star status overpositioned.

This I think is the most common mistake you're going to make, over-positioning yourself too much. You are emphasizing too long and too insistently your star status, bragging and being cocky too much. In short, being overbearing will not attract her at all, but will repel her a lot. So be careful, you must position yourself as a star, but with humility, as an anecdote, as something you have, but you don't want to boast about it.

Star status subpositioned.

If you really mention your stardom but don't sell it well as something fantastic, then she will think it's a pretty normal thing and you won't enjoy that star status. You must sell it but without boasting, she has to be aware of the power of this stardom.

Arrogant kindness.

Nor can we be kind and paternal with arrogance, but with an attitude of true affection and consideration; not cocky and looking down on us. The boastfulness and cockiness we already did in the confrontation, in everything else we have to eliminate these actions as much as possible.

Practical examples.

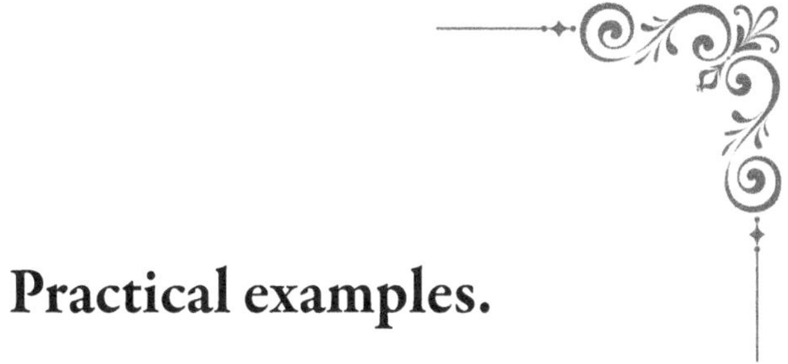

I am going to put here some examples that demonstrate that any of these methods, in any of their versions, work.

I really think that this book the EDP method is a new **Bible of seduction** that should be read, reread, and assimilated perfectly, as well as put into practice.

With these five methods of seduction there can be no woman who can resist the charms of the sexeducer.

Now I have also filmed three seduction courses. In them I go out talking to the camera explaining each and every one of the issues related to seduction. These video courses are on hotmart and all the existing audiovisual platforms.

At the moment the courses are:

Master Seduction.

The charmer.

Fucking power.

There will be two more courses coming soon.

I'll move on to the story of how I applied this.

Well, I once went to a place as a seduction coach to do some work. I spent several days there, and in the evenings I interacted with the women.

When asked what I do for a living, I would say without hesitation, "I am a seduction coach, I am a seducer, I have come here to work on this.

I showed myself as a seduction star and showed no interest in seducing these women. I was a little bit disgusted by what I was doing and I confronted her, I got into it with her, I told her what I really thought, not giving a fuck whether or not I hit on her, I was even a little bit nasty.

Then I realized that I had gone too far and I made up for it with charm, valuation and even a little gallantry. I noticed that this confrontation had an effect, the next day she was calling me wanting to meet, I went but I did not feel like being around her and instead of seducing her I went home and left her forgotten, she continued calling but finally I did not consider her suitable and left her without closing because I fucking felt like it.

With other women, as soon as I told them I was a seduction coach, their eyes widened like saucers and they were amazed and enthusiastic about it. With this image as a seduction star, an image that you can also have with the Master Seduction course, the girls flirted with me, approached me, and some even harassed me a little.

I told the most interesting one that I wanted her to be my manager and to manage several issues for me there. I told her - I'm the star, your star, the manager has to take **care of all her** star's needs.

I don't know if it was because of the great charm, or because of the star position in her head, the fact is that they worked wonderfully and this girl named by me "my manager" was every day suggesting me things to do, places to go and so on.

Of course I hooked up with my manager and things were going well, but little by little she became more and more distant and cold and it got to a point where she didn't even want to kiss me. This seemed to me a very serious offense and I confronted her. I told her that I didn't feel like seeing her anymore, that she was no longer my manager, that I didn't feel well valued, and that I didn't go with women who didn't value me.

I liked myself, I was hard and I abandoned her, I went around for several days on my own without paying any attention to her, saying no to her proposals and not seeing her. I went out with the other one that I also rejected because I didn't like her.

A few days after this confrontation with the manager she started to be much more open, receptive, affectionate and devoted. I re-friended her and she finally confessed that she had a boyfriend and that's why she was behaving that way, but that she liked me.

Then I began to be kinder, to treat her better, to go with her more, and little by little she gave herself up to total consummation.

And so by being a star, being sincere, saying what you do, confronting what you don't like, and being kind, loving, nice and protective, I swept that place and had an apotheosis triumph that could have been many more if I had dedicated myself a little more.

Inner set for use with EDP methods.

Well, here we are going to do the mental screen as usual, we are going to visualize ourselves not as a person who seduces, but as **the star of seduction**, the Master Seduction that has women excited. We are going to see ourselves telling them that we are seducers, that we are a Master Seduction, that we are graduates, that we are the star, that we want her to have a great time, that we are not going to use our seduction arts on her, that we are going to be kind.

You can imagine her being surprised, making the face of a shocked girl, positively impressed by this statement.

Then you look charismatic, protective, loving and caring playing with your protégé.

Visualize everything perfectly.

And now as a novelty, once you have finished the visualization, you are going to write on a piece of paper how you feel, how you have seen this girl, and you, write a few sentences about how you feel and what you have seen on your mental screen.

Then, every day, you will read these phrases, which will empower you and make you feel like the star of seduction.

Keep this paper in front of you every night and read it several times before going to bed and when you wake up. You read it every day until you really believe that you are the star of seduction.

Interactions.

To seduce in large quantities you will have to have a lot of interactions, this is super important, so relate every fucking day with many people, get out of the house, go to events, conferences, exhibitions, participate in activities, get into groups of all kinds and maximize the new people you talk to every day.

Many of the possibilities come from an intense social life. It's also easier and less awkward than cold approaching. Be someone with a huge social life and you will be able to put all these methods to good use.

Go for it!

End.

Seducing is not only about getting the girl, it's about enjoying the process, it's about feeling magnificent and special, therefore these new EDP and JD methods empower you and make you feel great moments.

If you put them into practice well, you will be very successful, if you do it wrong it will be a disaster, it depends on you, that what you say is coherent with what you think, that you have total confidence in you. Be great and shine, remember that you are the star of seduction.

This is all a game, so,

Let's play!

Also by John Danen

Seduction 5.0
S.A.X.
Chicas complicadas
Seducción 5.0
El libro del tonto
Macho Alpha
Macho alpha extracto
La seducción después de la pandemia
Terriblemente atractivo
Seducción 5.1
Sedução 5.1
How to be Cool and Attractive
Sedução. Avançada. X.
Garotas complicadas
¡Basta de ser buen chico! Sé un chico malo.
El método JD. El método de seducción de John Danen
El arte de agradarte a ti mismo
¡Basta ya de abusos! ¡Defiéndete!
Enought with the abuse! Defend yourself!
Máster en seducción
Las mujeres. El amor. Y el sexo.
Supera la dependencia emocional
Atrae mujeres con masculinidad
JD Absoluta seducción
El fracaso del amor

Entender a las mujeres
La vida del seductor sinvergüenza y encantador.
El arte de la dureza
Terrivelmente atraente
Deixe de ser um bom da fita! Seja um mauzão.
Superar a dependência emocional
A arte de se agradar
Pare o abuso! Defenda-se!
O fracasso do amor.
O método JD
Don´t Be a Good Boy! Be a Badass
Complicated girls
The Art of Pleasing Yourself
Duro y Sinvergüenza
Mestre en sedução
JD Method
The Failure of Love. The Trap of Serious Relationships
Master in Seduction
A. S. X. Advanced. Seduction. X
Women. Love. Sex
How to Become a Real Man. Be an Alpha Male
Attract Women with Masculinity
JD Absolut Seductión
Understanding Women
The Life of the Shameless and Charming Seducer.
The Art of Toughness
Tough and Shameless
Überwindung der Emotionalen Abhängigkeit
Maître en séduction
Schrecklich Attraktiv
Surmonter la Dépendance Émotionnelle
L'art de la dureté
Die Kunst der Zähigkeit

Hör auf, ein guter Junge zu sein, sei ein böser Junge
Assez D'être un Bon Garçon ! Sois un Mauvais Garçon.
Die Kunst, sich Selbst zu Gefallen
Dur et sans Vergogne
Hart im Nehmen und Schamlos
L'art de se Plaire à soi-Même
Das Scheitern der Liebe
L'échec de L'amour.
Meister der Verführung
Die JD-Methode
Maestro di Seduzione
Terriblement Attrayant
La Méthode JD
Capire le donne
Compreendendo as Mulheres
Comprendre les Femmes
Die Frauen Verstehen
Les Filles Compliquées
Komplizierte Mädchen
JD Séduction Absolue
La Vie du Séducteur Charmant et sans Vergogne
Les Femmes. L'amour. Et le Sexe.
Mâle Alpha
S.A.X.
V.F.X.
Donne. Amore. E il sesso.
Ragazze Complicate
Superare la Dipendenza Emotiva
Seduzione. Avanzata. X.
Dark Seducción
Il Fallimento Dell'amore.
Il Metodo JD
Alphamännchen

Atrair Mulheres com Masculinidade
Attirare le donne con la Mascolinità
Attirer les Femmes par la Masculinité
Mit Männlichkeit Frauen Anziehen
Frauen. Liebe. Und Sex.
L'arte di Piacere a se Stessi
Mulheres. Amor. E Sexo.
JD Seduzione Assoluta
JD Absolute Verführung
JD Sedução Absoluta
Das Leben des charmanten, schamlosen Verführers
Smettila di Fare il Bravo Ragazzo! Essere un Cattivo Ragazzo.
La Vita del Seduttore Affascinante e Spudorato
A Vida do Sedutor Encantador e sem Vergonha
Macho Alfa
Uomo Alfa
Séduction 5.0
Verführung 5.0
Seduzione 5.0
Duro e Senza Vergogna
Duro e Sem Vergonha
L'arte della Durezza
A Arte da Dureza
The Fool's Book
Das Buch der Dummköpfe
Il Libro dei Pazzi
O Livro do Tolo
Dark Seduction
Dunkle Verführung
Sedução Escura
Dark Seduction
Seduzione Oscura
Le livre du fou

Como materializar lo que deseas con el fxxxxxx power
Como materializar o que você quer com o Fxxxxxx Power
El ángel Sex-terminador
El seductor vampiro
O Vampiro Sedutor
Sex-Terminating Angel
The Vampire Seducer
How to Materialize What You Want With The Fxxxxxx Power
El camino del maestro
Il vampiro seduttore
O camiño do mestre
La via del maestro
Der verführerische Vampir
Le sedusant vampire
Der Weg des Meisters
La voie du maître de la séduction
Master's Path
Come materializzare ciò che si desidera con il Fxxxxxx Power
Wie Sie Ihre Wünsche verwirklichen können mit dem Fxxxxxx Power
El método EDP
O método EDP
The E.D.P. Method
Comment matérialiser ce que vous désirez avec le Fxxxxxx power

About the Author

Español.

Soy un hombre vividor y divertido que busca el lado bueno de las cosas siempre.

Mi experiencia es el campo de las relaciones personales y de la seducción. Por eso tras dedicarme larguísimas décadas a ello, quiero trasmitir mis conocimientos. Para que las nuevas generaciones tengan unos conceptos que les den una ventaja competitiva sostenible y poderosa en el campo del amor.

Quiero ayudarte a a conseguir tus metas.

Portugués.

Sou um homem animado, e divertido, que sempre procura o lado bom das coisas.

Minha experiência está no campo das relações pessoais e da sedução. É por isso que, após décadas de dedicação a ela, quero transmitir meus conhecimentos.

Quero ajudá-los a alcançar seus objetivos.

Inglés

I am a lively and fun man, who always looks for the good side of things.

My experience is in the field of personal relationships and seduction. That is why, after decades of dedicating myself to it, I want to pass on my knowledge. So that the new generations have concepts that give them a sustainable and powerful competitive advantage in the field of love.

I want to help you achieve your goals

Français Je suis un homme vif et drôle qui cherche toujours le bon côté des choses.

Mon expérience se situe dans le domaine des relations personnelles et de la séduction. C'est pourquoi, après m'y être consacré pendant des décennies, je veux transmettre mes connaissances. Pour que les nouvelles générations disposent de concepts qui leur donnent un avantage concurrentiel durable et puissant dans le domaine de l'amour.

Je veux vous aider à atteindre vos objectifs.